Golden Hours

COLOUR GIFT BOOKS

Perfect gift books at little more than the cost of a greeting card. A completely new series illustrated throughout in *superb full colour.* Each 32 pages.

LOOKING FORWARD
BESIDE THE STILL WATERS
LIGHT FOR TODAY
THOUGHTS GO HOME
TAKE COMFORT
NATURE'S CATHEDRAL
THE RHYTHM OF THE SEASONS
RING IN THE NEW

THE GLORY BEYOND
GIVE LIFE TIME
THE HARBOUR OF CONTENTMENT
QUIET THOUGHTS FOR THE QUIET HOUR
THE LAMP OF CHEERFULNESS
THE GARDEN THROUGH THE YEAR
OUT INTO THE SUNSHINE
THE HAVEN OF THE HEART

THE QUIET HOUR Series

HOUSE OF DREAMS
SOMEWHERE OVER THE HILL
THE BEST IS YET TO COME
COME HAPPY DAY
WINGS OF THE MORNING
THROUGH THE YEAR

THE QUIET CORNER
THE QUIET HOUR
QUIET MOMENTS
ROSES FOR REMEMBRANCE
PASSING CLOUDS
HARBOURS OF HAPPINESS

ILLUSTRATED GIFT BOOKS

GIVE ME A QUIET CORNER

Based on Patience Strong's own philosophy of life, offering thoughts of hope, contentment and faith. These verses with their evocative accompanying photographs make this book one that every admirer will turn to for inspiration in time of need.

THE HARVEST OF A QUIET EYE
THE TAPESTRY OF TIME
HOMES AND GARDENS

DAILY READINGS

THE BIRTHDAY BOOK
THE BEDSIDE BOOK
THE FRIENDSHIP BOOK
THE MORNING WATCH
THE GLORY OF THE GARDEN
THE GIFT BOOK
THE KINGDOM WITHIN

LIFE IS FOR LIVING

Patience Strong's study of practical psychology.

Golden Hours
PATIENCE STRONG

FREDERICK MULLER LIMITED
LONDON

First published in Great Britain 1952
by Frederick Muller Limited, London
with gravure illustrations.

This edition, with new illustrations
throughout, 1977.

ISBN 0 584 10746 3

Colour Photographs by Colour Library International Ltd.
CLI House, Coombe Road, New Malden, Surrey

Printed in Spain

Golden Hours
PATIENCE STRONG

Joys and Sorrows

When the little worlds we build come tumbling down about our ears — When we look upon the ruin of the hopes of happier years . . . It is then that we are challenged, forced to look into the heart — searching for sufficient faith to make another better start.

Happiness must blend with sorrow. Many changes Time must bring. We are strengthened and enriched by mingled joy and suffering. We have never truly lived or touched the inner core of life — until we've tasted sweet and bitter, bliss and anguish, peace and strife.

High Standards

Be true to what is best in you and set the standard high. Be loyal to your vision. Do not waver or deny the truths you've tried and proved, the lofty faith you have professed. Be true in every detail to the finest and the best.

The battle between right and wrong goes on unceasingly. Though none be there to witness your defeat or victory, the obligation is the same, the moral law still stands. Be true. Come through with conscience clear, a good name and clean hands.

Landscapes of the Mind

The landscape changes overnight, the landscape of the mind. Shadows steal into the hollows where the deep streams wind. Mists of doubt obscure the summits of the peak of hope. Thoughts of fear like veils of rain blot out the upward slope.

But this is Life . . . No day the same. How dull the world would be — if nothing ever touched the heart or changed the scenery . . . Through the windows of our dreams we see a varied view: gloom and glory, storm and sunshine, skies of black and blue.

3

The Shallows and the Deep

Quiet and shallow are the waters where the leafy willows sway — Yet this little winding river flowing gently on its way — is going out to meet the sea and swell the ocean's rolling tide. The stream will widen to embrace the mighty waves where great ships ride.

Uneventful life may seem, a narrow stream of nights and days — Yet somewhere in the future it will open into broader ways. Every soul in God's own time is called unto its destiny — to steer its course alone upon the waters of Eternity.

The Old Inn

Many a weary traveller has seen the swinging sign — and halted on his journey here for bread or beer or wine. Many a pilgrim on the road has seen the friendly light — has found a welcome at the door and lodging for the night.

Men were sitting round the hearth beneath the oaken beams — when Shakespeare walked in Stratford town and dreamed his golden dreams . . . This little English wayside inn was old in history — when good Queen Bess was on the throne and Drake was on the sea.

5

Our Precious Countryside

Pretty country cottages in little English lanes — with white-washed walls and cosy thatch and lattice window-panes — never look so lovely as when roses bright and gay — cover them with glory on a golden summer's day.

Time is on the march today with swift gigantic stride. How can we preserve and save our precious countryside? Will our children walk these lanes and see as we have seen — Cottage gardens, flowery banks, old trees and fields of green.

The Mark of Destiny

He was made for love and laughter, useful work and happy life. Not for hate and violence, for bloodshed and for bitter strife . . . He was made to play good cricket and to walk the countryside — free to take the morning road with merry heart and swinging stride.

Yet he did not live to reap the harvests of the fields of Time. Not for him the fruit of manhood ripening to golden prime . . . Fate upon that clear young brow had put the mark of destiny. He was of the generation born to save humanity.

7

Treasures of Darkness

There are treasures to be found in places desolate. Hidden gold in secret mines. Things fine and true and great — are often born of bitterness of pain and poverty. Many a lovely thing was fashioned in adversity.

If we dwelt like heavenly beings in perpetual light — We should never see the glory of the starry night . . . If Joy were our companion all along a broad bright way — we should dance our way through life forgetting how to pray.

Waiting for Another Spring

It is not until the tree is stripped of all its leafy green — that the eye can see its form, the naked branches smooth and clean; the grace and structure of the boughs, the shapely limbs, the trunk, the bark. It stands revealed in all its beauty, strong and lovely, black and stark.

Sorrow comes to everyone to strip the soul and lay it bare. But the faithful have deep roots — Through pain and anguish grief and care, like the trees in Wintertime where no leaf stirs and no birds sing — They stand unmoved, believing, hoping . . . waiting for another Spring.

9

The Tapestry of Time

Life works out a pattern on the tapestry of Time. The threads of hope, of love and grief, of fear and faith sublime — of happiness and bitterness, of joy and misery — are stitched into the great design of human destiny.

Within so vast a frame our tiny patch we cannot see. Too close we stand to trace the pattern on the tapestry — But someday looking from afar perhaps we shall behold — Our little bit of the design, our own small thread of gold.

In England Now

In England now the blackcap sings and martins dart on tireless wings — about their nests in cottage eaves, behind a latticework of leaves . . . Across the meadows there has rolled — a rippling tide of green and gold. The flower is on the apple bough — And lilac blooms . . . In England now.

The hawthorn whitens once again along the hedges in the lane — and gay is every garden plot with tulip and forget-me-not. The herds in quiet pastures stand, and Beauty is upon the land — as if basked in God's own smile. This dear, this sweet, this blessed Isle.

The Fairest Sight in all the World

Silver-winged above the earth men travel through the sky. We are told that in the future everyone will fly, but we who are an island race must not forget the sea. Ships have made us what we are and shaped our destiny.

Ships! . . . The magic word evokes the thought of wind and tide. Docks and harbours, blue horizons, oceans deep and wide. Mighty vessels bound for lands romantic and remote. The fairest sight in all the world: a lovely ship afloat.

To the Bereaved

Trouble not your weary eyes with gazing after vanished dreams. Follow not into the past the echo of forgotten themes. Burden not the memory with too much dark and heavy grief. God is good and offers you the balm that gives the heart relief.

The dead have passed into His care. What more could we desire to know? They have travelled on ahead unto the place where all must go . . . Links with heaven we possess through those dear souls beyond our sight. Through their passing we too move a little nearer to the Light.

The Spendthrift

Nature now is minting gold, new gold that shines and gleams — celandines upon the bank and kingcups by the streams. Dandelions in the meadows thrusting boldly up. Garden crocus opening her dainty golden cup.

On the heaths and commons furze in flower and budding broom. Coltsfoot growing in the grasses with its yellow bloom . . . In the orchards woods and parks the daffodils unfold. Spendthrift Nature scatters wide her newly minted gold.

14

Sweet is the Dream

Sweet is the dream that comes upon the tides of memory, like a lovely ship afloat upon a golden sea. The dream in which my heart recaptures Love's first April mood. The dream that never fails to come to haunt my solitude.

Waking, sleeping, it is there, the dream that has no end. The thought of you, my dear companion, and my soul's true friend . . . From the evils of the world, from sorrow and distress — I escape into my dream, and there find happiness.

The Sun is Old

The sun is old, as old as Time, but every dawn is new. The light of all created life has burned in heaven's blue — since that first sweet daybreak when the sun sent down its rays — on a green and sinless world of fresh untrodden ways.

The sun is old, beyond the span of mortal reckoning — Yet every golden sunrise is a new and glorious thing. Every time the morning glory lights your window-pane — It can be a new beginning. Life can start again.

16

The Ship Goes Sailing On

The ship goes down below the line dividing sea and sky. The dim shape passes from the vision of the human eye, disappearing out of sight beyond the range of view. Yet it still goes sailing on into the boundless blue.

At death the spirit passes out into Eternity — Like a ship that sinks below the far line of the sea. Though upon the shore of Life we watch it fade from sight — Somewhere it goes sailing on into the morning light.

So Long as Love Abides

They laid him where he fell in battle, far away from me — where I cannot plant his grave with flowers of memory . . . That last sweet solace is denied. An exile still he lies — underneath the alien stars of unfamilier skies.

Yet the part of him I loved, the spirit and the mind — is clothed in immortality and could not be confined . . . To the faithful death is life and no dark gulf divides. He will dwell within my heart so long as love abides.

Farmer's Dawn

Smell of porridge from the kitchen, kettle singing at the hearth. Sound of hooves, of stamping feet and wheels upon the rutted path. In the yard the voice of the cowmen bringing in the waiting herd. From a dark and dripping bush the first faint twitter of a bird.

Crust of frost upon the furrows. Frozen puddles in the lane. Man and beast from sleep awaking, turning to the earth again. Talk of ploughing and of planting, fruit and hay and milk and corn. Chanticleer with cry triumphant heralding the farmer's dawn.

19

The Cell

Say not there is nothing left when you have suffered grievous loss. Say not that you see no light beyond the shadow of your cross . . . There is always something more to hope and pray and struggle for. Who knows where the road may lead or what the future holds in store?

Say not that your life is finished when your dearest ones depart — Don't leave others in the cold outside the gateway of your heart. Come forth from the cell of sorrow. Time is precious. Life is brief. There are those who love and need you. Sojourn not too long with grief.

Pray for Them

If you're feeling weary with your burden and the strain — Think of those compelled to lie upon a bed of pain. Call to mind the sufferers who cannot work or play — shut apart from all that makes life rich and good and gay.

Not for them the stir and struggle of a busy day — the adventures and encounters of the crowded way . . . Pray for them, and grateful be that you are on your feet — with duties to be tackled, work to do and friends to meet.

There in Spirit

Now the bright-eyed daisies open and the buttercups unfold — spreading on the watermeads a dazzling cloth of fairy gold . . . White clouds sail the blue of heaven, white herds graze beside the stream. Far from home, yet there in spirit, I, in exile, dream this dream.

In my fancy I am leaning on the old gate in the lane — seeing Maytime come to England and the fields turn gold again . . . Gazing at the yellow pastures where the silver waters thread — Listening with the old sweet wonder to a skylark overhead.

All Will Come Right

When things get all tangled and nothing looks straight — don't get in a fluster and rail against Fate — If you've the faith and the patience to wait . . . All will come right in the end.

When castles have tumbled don't fret or complain. Get up and get going and start out again — your dreams to achieve and your goal to attain . . . All will come right in the end.

When lost and perplexed and uncertain you feel — wondering where and to whom to appeal — Be true to yourself and your highest ideal and all will come right in the end.

23

The Old Towns by the Sea

Men have walked these huddled streets for centuries untold — have seen the sea through crooked cracks where gables grey and old lean above the narrow alleys, blotting out the sky. And still they tread the ancient lanes and watch the ships go by.

From the cliffs above the roofs the streets come tumbling down — falling steeply to the harbour of the little town . . . Let us take a solemn vow that in the years to be — No vandal hand shall touch and spoil our old towns by the sea.

Thoughts Go Home

Thoughts go home unbidden when we're somewhere far away. Thoughts need no compelling, off they wander night or day to seek the places and the faces dear unto the heart — the spot where all our journeys end, and all roads end and start.

Thoughts go back. They know the way. They need no goad or guide — to cross the hills and rivers or the oceans that divide. And though with friends we may abide, wherever we may roam — To the place of heart's desire thoughts turn . . . Love leads them home.

Our Memories

Time brings many changes, joys and sorrows, smiles and tears — But memories grow sweeter with the passing of the years . . . Those whom we have loved and lost draw near and seem to press — round about us in our moments of unhappiness.

We miss the loving handclasp and the voice we knew so well. We miss the living breathing presence more than we can tell . . . We miss the dear companionship a little more each day — But God gives us our memories that none can take away.

Reading

A book's a good companion for dark days or for bright. It speeds Time's leaden footsteps and puts our cares to flight . . . A book's a friend and solace when other friends have passed. Your favourite book will cheer you and charm you to the last.

Though other pleasures vanish the joy of this remains. The mind is led, enchanted, down green and winding lanes. Imagination lingers at inns of quietness — and from their golden windows the wide earth we possess . . . Upon the printed pages in thought we travel far — across the deepest ocean, beyond the brightest star.

Sons of the Sea

There's salt in the veins of a Briton. There's salt in the blood and the bone.
In places remote and romantic the seed of their race they have sown.

In peace they have sailed the wide waters — in search of new worlds and
new ways — Have pushed back the distant horizons in grand and
adventurous days.

In war they have challenged the tyrant — upholding the rights of the free
— Have battled their way into glory and proved themselves sons of the sea.

On Holy Ground

The mind and spirit are enriched and on the heart a blessing falls — when we stand on holy ground and kneel within the hallowed walls where men through untold centuries have worshipped God in prayer and praise. Here the soul receives refreshment as to Him our thoughts we raise.

Saints have died a martyr's death this privilege to win for us — this dear and precious liberty, this freedom sweet and glorious . . . To gather in some sacred place the beauty of the Word to hear. To declare our Christian creed and name our Saviour without fear.

Decisions

You can get on or can stay where you are. Stop in one place or strike out and go far. Sit in a corner or follow a star . . . It is for you to decide.

You can go under or rise with the tide. Shutter your windows or open them wide. Fate can defeat you or Fate be defied . . . It is for you to decide.

You can go higher, can climb or can fall, living your life in a world big or small. You can be something or nothing at all . . . It is for you to decide.

Home

Home! . . . It's just a simple word but oh how much it means: things we've come to know and love amidst familiar scenes, the memory of which we treasure, every stick and stone. Our corner of the universe, a haven of our own.

Home! . . . Our bit of God's good earth, the dearest bit of all. The spot where our affections centre — whether big or small, it stands for all the precious things we've worked and struggled for. The heart's abode, the little world behind our own front door.

31

Love's Bequest

Never will you come again with laughing lips and shining eyes. Nevermore will you return to walk beneath our English skies — for you are sleeping far away the last sleep of the brave and true. Your resting place a battlefield where none can come to mourn for you.

But for my comfort you have left a rich and lasting legacy: the secret wealth of recollection and of dearest memory. This you have bequeathed to me, a love undying, deep and fond — to be my peace, my hope, my joy in this world . . . and the world beyond.

Sun on Stone

Hope is like the sun upon the threshold of the heart. A glow lights up the inner room. The shadows fall apart and rising to unlatch the door we cast all fear away — as we venture out into the brightness of the day.

Hope is like a ray of sunlight falling on grey stone. The heart is warmed. We're tempted out to take the road alone — out towards a broad horizon where the sky is gold — with promise of the love of God and blessings manifold.

Hearthside Thoughts

Youth steals away with the vanishing years. Much is forgotten as older we grow. Songs once remembered grow faint in our ears. Outlines get hazy as onward we go.

But friendship remains. Love endures to the last. In the quiet hours we remember dear names. Ghosts haunt our hearths. Happy thoughts of the past. Faces and pictures appear in the flames.

God gives us memories for our Decembers. Something to comfort when darkness descends. Things to recall as we dream by the embers. Heart-warming thoughts of old times and old friends.

Cottage in the Hills

In a cup between the hills a little cottage dreams — a place of leaning gables, timbered walls and oaken beams. A spot to set the heart upon, a fairy-story place. A human sort of cottage with a smile upon its face.

Is not this the joy of England? Unexpectedly — we turn a bend and find that we are back in history. Little old-world cottages in snug seclusion stand — all about the hills and valleys of our lovely land.

Pictures in the Heart

There are pictures in the heart: the things we see when lost in dreams: churches nestling in green valleys, grey old mills by quiet streams. Field and forest, moor and meadow, silver lake and stately pine — waving corn and fields of harvest flowing to the sky's broad line.

Flocks in Dorset pastures grazing. Lochs of Scotland, Yorkshire dales. Cliffs of Devon, Cornish harbours and the purple peaks of Wales . . . Kentish orchards, downs of Sussex rolling to the Channel foam. Living pictures in the heart: the unforgotten scenes of home.

Music

Music is a language universal in its scope — expressing every shade and tone of human fear and hope . . . Bliss and grief and all that lies between those two extremes — sorrow, wonder, exaltation and unspoken dreams.

All mankind can know and grasp and understand these things: the fingers on the keyboard and the bow upon the strings. Men need no interpreters their message to impart — when they speak through music in the language of the heart.

Someone There

It cannot be that they are dead, though passed beyond our touch and call. It cannot be that they have gone from those who loved them best of all . . . They could not leave us lost and lonely in the bitter wind of grief. They would not leave us groping in the darkness of our unbelief.

They come to us in many forms along the lanes of Memory. But we are earthbound, limited, too deaf to hear, too blind to see. Yet sometimes when the house is still there comes a step upon the stair . . . a warmth of joy about the heart, a sudden sense of someone there.

Homeland

Where the heart is, that is Homeland — be it north south east or west . . .
Where our thoughts are, that's our own land, and the place we love the best.

It's for this the soldier fights, the exile dreams, the poet sings. It's for this
that men have done heroic and immortal things.

Where Shadows End

When we stand amongst the shadows it is chill and cold — but where the sunshine meets the shadow there's an edge of gold . . . Just outside the blackest patches it is warm and bright. From the darkness of the shade we step into the light.

Life is not a path of glory. Troubles come our way. Shadows fall across the road upon the brightest day . . . But at last we reach a place where hopes with sorrows blend: the golden edges of the sunshine . . . where the shadows end.

The House with Many Windows

A selfish life is like a house without a window-pane — a house from which the eye can see no sunshine and no rain — No outward view, no glimpse of heaven, only solid walls — a house that's like a prison where no gleam of sunlight falls.

A selfless life is like a house with windows everywhere — from which the world is seen with all its joy and all its care . . . Windows open to the winds of hope and sympathy. Windows lit with shining lamps of faith and charity.

41

Leaf Language

What are the birches whispering? What does the old oak say? What do the beech trees talk about all through the night and day? Huddled together secretly — murmuring mystic words. Leaning towards each other and gossiping with the birds. I wish that I knew the language. I wish that I understood — the things that the trees are saying down in the deep green wood.

Leave Your Worries

Leave your worries by the wayside. Do not take them on your back. Why go burdened, stumbling, stooping on life's rough and stony track?

You will get there all the sooner if you drop that heavy load. Bent with care you will miss the sights and half the fun along the road.

Make a pile of all your worries — Dump them, leave them, let them be . . . Then go forth with head uplifted feeling lighter, brighter, free.

On the Bridge

When you come to a lovely grey old bridge that spans a sparkling stream
— you feel you want to linger there and watch the waters gleam . . . You may
be in a hurry and reluctant to delay — knowing all the time you should be
going on your way, but something in the sound of water purling over stones,
full of lilting laughter and of secret undertones — makes you stand
enchanted, drifting idly in a dream — fascinated by the fairy music of the
stream.

There is a Milestone

There is a milestone on life's path that brings us to another start — where brighter vistas open out, where clouds grow light and break apart . . . There is a spot on every road where ruts give way to smooth green ways — the place that marks a new beginning and the hope of fairer days.

Are you weary with the journey? Does your burden seem too great? Are you fighting uphill battles, struggling with a hostile fate? The milestone at the turning point may be a few steps round the bend. Courage! This may be the place where joys return and troubles end.

The Pathways
of the Heart

There are pathways in the heart, old tracks that Time has made — where countless dreams have left their mark and many thoughts have strayed — All the old familiar trails of happy memory — are hedged about with flowers of friendship and felicity.

All paths lead at last to you along the well-worn way — where Love has left its footprint hour by hour and day by day. No matter where my dreams may stray or where my thoughts may roam — It's never long before I strike the path that takes me home.

By the Lily Pool

From the hidden mud-clogged roots have come these lovely things —
delicate and perfect with exquisite colourings . . . Marvelling, I've watched
and seen the folded buds unclose: ivory and alabaster, gold and white and
rose.

Pale upon the sunlet pool the water lilies lie — in the shadows and the clouds
of the reflected sky. Round the green isles of the leaves the dragonflies in
flight — set the air a-quivering with streaks of rainbow light.

The Church Tower

The centuries have come and gone above the old church tower, and o'er the green and quiet fields the clock has chimed the hour . . . It stands, a fortress of the spirit, calm, impregnable. Undisturbed by time or tumult, strong and beautiful.

Grey against the English sky a symbol and a sign — of powers that are invisible and things that are divine . . . A monument triumphant to the Life, the Truth the Way. A mute but mighty challenge to the evils of our day.

48

Time Stands Still

Time stands still in the forest. The old trails wind and thread — amongst the oaks and beeches where mighty branches spread — above the glens and glades where, undisturbed, birds come and go — through the tangled thickets where the silver brooklets flow.

Time stands still in the forest. It might be Chaucer's day — or Shakespeare might come wandering along the woodland way. No mark of man's abiding, no human sign intrudes — upon the ancient silence of sylvan solitudes.

49

The Search for Happiness

Happiness is incidental, something that we find — growing like unlooked for flowers down byways of the mind . . . Happiness is like the sunshine on a winter's day — stealing unexpectedly through skies of cloudy grey.

If we seek it for ourselves on selfish pleasures bent — we never seem to find the gate that leads to heart's content . . . But if we think of others and ourselves a little less — we discover that we've found the key to happiness.

The Harvest Scene

Old as man yet ever lovely, pleasing to the eye: the pattern of the harvest fields beneath the August sky . . . The golden sheaves of gathered corn in long unbroken rows. Like a picture breathing peace, fulfilment and repose.

Much has gone into the making of this quiet scene — ploughing up the frosted earth on mornings bleak and keen — money and machinery and human diligence — The sunshine and the rainfall and the Lord's good providence.

51

Great Men

What is greatness? How do men achieve this quality — and win an honoured place upon the scroll of history? Not alone by wisdom, wit or work of hand and brain. Greatness lies beyond all these within the soul's domain.

Great men with a simple faith pursue a noble aim — seeking not for worldly prizes, glory, praise or fame . . . Following an inward vision, humbly, earnestly. Servants of the will of God and of humanity.

The Next Step

    We can't retrace our steps through life. We must go on, we can't turn back. We must leave the past behind and walk the unfamiliar track . . . The next step is the one that takes us out along the unknown way. This the road that we must travel, not the roads of yesterday.

    Every step into the future is a venture in the dark — on a path where there may be no friendly sign, no guiding mark . . . Fear not. Take the next step forward. Walk with faith into the night. There is One who walks beside you in the darkness and the light.

Under the Leaves

In the lane and on the common, in the garden and the glade. In the woods and in the orchards autumn carpets have been laid — On the hills and in the hollows thickly now the leaves are spread, woven into lovely patterns, gold and russet, bronze and red.

It is not a shroud of death to cover ruin and decay. Nothing dies though all things change. The leaves may fall and fade away — but life goes on beneath the surface, dormant bulbs and roots unseen — will awaken with the Spring and clothe the earth in living green.

54

Pilgrims to the Sunrise

All who seek to serve the Master, walking in His way — look with hope and faith undaunted to the glorious day, when the nations spent with war, by strife and sorrow torn — seek the promise of the glow of God's millennial Dawn.

All who labour for His sake are marching to the light. Pilgrims to the Sunrise pressing onward through the night. Bringing news of man's salvation and the world's rebirth — Tidings of the coming of His Kingdom upon earth.

Built to Last

The ancient buildings of the past were made by craftsmen, built to last. Throughout old England one can see these monuments of history. Cottage, manor, church and farm — things of dignity and charm. Spires and gables, beams and domes. Cosy inns and stately homes.

When we come to build anew — May our work be good and true. No more cheap and shoddy ways. Building for the future days, let us learn from those who planned and laboured here with heart and hand: the builders of an age now gone. Time passes, but good work lives on.

Our Needs

Our needs are many, we who walk the rough and busy roads of life. We need stout shoes to climb the hills and weapons for the constant strife . . . We need the warmth of hearth and home, a place to rest, a roof, a bed. We need a lamp when darkness comes, and food upon the table spread.

The soul, too, has necessities: the need for human sympathy — for kindliness, for happiness, for faith and hope and charity. And more than all we need God's love. Without it we are poor indeed. The daily gift of His forgiveness is our great and deepest need.

As God Sends Spring

As God sends Spring at winter's end and birds return to build again — As dark woods quicken into green beneath the kiss of April's rain — So shall I wake one happy day and feel the pulse of life anew, looking out with fearless eyes towards a broader brighter view . . . Discovering forgotten dreams, and happiness so long denied — learning how to live again by many sorrows purified . . . As new sap rises in the bough and bursts the folded buds apart — so will hope bring forth her flowers and joy return unto my heart.